BRAIN *friendly*

Contents

Pictures (Side A) / Exercises (Side B)

Illustrations by Mark Fletcher

BRAIN-friendly is the registered trade mark™ of Mark Fletcher and Richard Munns

TEACHING NOTES

Using **Pictures of English Tenses - Level 1**

● Photocopy Side A for **oral practice** in the target structure.
Photocopy Side B for **written follow up.**

● The Teaching Notes give you **'prompt' questions** to generate the correct structures – and also **answers** to exercises.

● **Pictures of English Tenses - Level 1** concentrates on 4 key structures.
Each structure is consistently **linked with a colour**.
Present Simple (Dark Blue) & **Present Continuous** (Light Blue).
Past Simple (Brown) ... Autumn leaves ? Burnt Toast?
Future (Yellow) – a nice bright sunny future for everyone!

● Use these colours consistently so students quickly become familiar with them.

● The names in the picture drills, i.e. <u>BILL BROWN</u> (PAST Tense) reinforce this association.

● Students now have a "right hemisphere", colour-based system for identifying and using tenses.

The BRAIN *friendly*™ colour code for tenses

1 **Present Simple** – Dark Blue
2 **Present Continuous** – Light Blue
3 **Past Simple** – Brown
4 **Future** – Yellow

*My uncle **painted** this in 1920*

① *I paint lots of houses every year*

② *I'm painting my kitchen light blue*

④ *Tomorrow **I'm going** to paint this clock yellow*

BRAIN-*friendly* tip:
The teacher can correct by simply holding up the appropriate coloured pen – and the colour prompts the student into self correction.

The colour code for tenses is further developed in **Pictures of English Tenses Level 2** and **Level 3**

TEACHING NOTES

Unit 1 'The BIG PICTURE'

This unit gives an overview of **Present, Past**, and **Future tenses.** Students may not be using all of the tenses actively – but a passive knowledge is vital. (It's like seeing the picture on the outside of the jigsaw puzzle box before you start fitting individual pieces together!) The conversations with their "fill in the blanks" space introduce learners to the basics of the tenses and also to the "colour families".

Exercise 1
'Missing' lines.
What do you do , Duncan Dark Blue?
I paint houses.
I'm painting my kitchen - light blue, of course.
Did you paint this picture, Bill?
No. My Uncle, Bertie Brown, painted it in 1920.
What are you going to do tomorrow, Yolanda?
I'm going to paint my clock yellow.

> **BRAIN-*friendly* tip:**
> *Introduce "Colour family" idea with coloured pens/pencils – enough for students to share. (Also have coloured sweets as an incentive! Smarties are very good).*

Unit 2 'To be' and 'to have' - Present Simple (Dark Blue). Practice with 2 key verbs.

Side A: (to be) am are is are are
(to have) have have has have have
Side B:
Exercise 1 am are is are are
Exercise 2 have have has have have
Exercise 3 Are am / Is is / Is isn't / Are are / Are aren't
Exercise 4 have / have / Does have doesn't / Do have do / Do have do
Dark Blue

> **BRAIN-*friendly* tip:**
> *Have music playing (gently) as students practise their grammar.*

Unit 3 'To go' and 'To like'. Present Simple. (Dark Blue) Similar to Unit 2, but with one irregular verb (to go) and one typical regular verb (to like).

Point out 3rd person singular – 's'

Side A go go goes go go / like like likes like like
Side B
Exercise 1 go / go / goes / go / go
Exercise 2 like / Do like don't / likes do / like / like don't
Exercise 3 do go / Do go don't / doesn't go goes / Do go don't / do go /
don't like do / Does like / like don't like
Dark Blue

> **BRAIN-*friendly* tip:**
> *Develop your personal 'handsignal' to remind students about final 's'*

Unit 4 'My day' - Present Simple (Dark Blue)

Tell the story (or elicit it from students). Use it as the basis for 'Does he...?' 'What time does he...?' 'Where/How does he...?' questions. Students can practise in pairs. When this pattern (and the vocabulary) is well established, one student (or one partner in the pair) becomes 'Duncan' and the other asks "Do you...?" "What time do you...?" "Where/How do you...?" questions based on the pictures. When that is established, move to 'real life' question and answer practice.

Exercise 1   On school days Duncan **Dark Blue** wakes up at 6.30. He has a wash. After that he gets dressed, and at 7.30 he has breakfast. He usually has cornflakes, bread and tea. He goes to school by bike and arrives at school at 8.45. He has lessons in the morning 'til lunch time. Lunch time at school is from 12.30 to 1.30. In the afternoons he has more lessons or plays sport. He normally arrives home (gets home) at half past four. Mum, Dad and Duncan Dark Blue have dinner at 8 pm. In the evenings Duncan does his homework, or watches TV, or meets his friends. They talk about their plans for the weekend.

Exercise 2   No. He has a wash.
He usually has cornflakes, bread, and tea.
He goes by bike.
He has lunch at school.
The journey (It) takes half an hour.
They have dinner at 8 p.m.

> **BRAIN-*friendly* tip:**
> *Class chants/hand taps the rhythm of 'When does he? Where does he? How does he do it?' – to internalise pattern.*

Exercise 3   "I usually get up..." etc.

TEACHING NOTES – B

TEACHING NOTES

Unit 5 'What is she doing?' - Present Continuous (Light Blue)

Exercise 1.1. He's watching TV. 2. She's taking the dog for a walk.
3. He's riding his bike. 4. He's driving a car.
5. They're playing basketball. 6. She's shopping.
7. He's cleaning shoes. 8. He's making a phone call.
9. They're talking. 10. He's sleeping. 11. He's swimming.
12. He's writing. 13. She's reading. 14. He's cutting the grass.
15. He's having a shower. 16. He's cooking.
17. He's climbing a mountain. 18. They're dancing.
19. He's singing. 20. He's getting on a bus.
21. He's getting off a bus. 22. She's listening to a cassette (walkman).
23. She's using a computer. 24. He's having a drink.
25. He's shouting. 26. He's crying.
The verbs which are not illustrated: **fight jog paint smoke**

BRAIN-*friendly* tip:
In teams. One representative mimes the actions and others guess it – "Are you listening to a cassette?".

Unit 6 'Usually, but......' Comparing Present Simple (Dark Blue) and Present Continuous (Light Blue)

Exercise 1
Dagmar: nurse wears helps works   No. She isn't. She's playing tennis
Duncan: is goes works reads   What is he doing? He is shopping.
Mrs. Blue: is a teacher   works teaches   She's on holiday (in a disco)
What is she doing? She is dancing.

Exercise 2
For example:
I learn English, I have lessons, I talk to my friends **(Dark Blue)**
I'm learning English, I'm writing, I'm sitting on a chair **(Light Blue)**

BRAIN-*friendly* tip:
Use thick dark and light blue pens to write master sentences on big posters. Keep them as 'peripherals'.

I paint lots of houses every year

I'm painting my kitchen light blue

Unit 7   **Bill Brown's holiday - Past Simple (Brown)**

BRAIN-*friendly* tip:
Individuals take turns to tell or mime 3 things from their holidays.

Exercise 1. I went shopping on Monday. I went skiing on Tuesday. I went dancing on Wednesday. I went fishing on Thursday. I went horse riding on Friday. I went hiking on Saturday.
The 3 things he didn't do? He didn't go climbing. He didn't go skate-boarding. He didn't go jogging.

Exercise 2. I stayed at the Sunny Hotel. I had (ate) some nice food. I went (rode) on a giant switchback. I played tennis. I bought some presents. I took some photos.

Unit 8   Betty's day out - Irregular Past (Brown)
When did Betty wake up? How did she get to the station? What did they do in the evening? etc.
Example conversation (Exercise 3)

Q.   Where did you go yesterday, Betty?
A.   I went to London.
Q.   Did you go alone?
A.   I went alone but I met a friend in London.
Q.   How did you get to London? Did you drive?
A.   No. I went by train.
Q.   What did you do there?
A.   We had lunch, then we bought some presents, then did some sightseeing.
Q.   Did you do anything interesting in the evening?
A.   Yes. We went to the cinema. Then I got the train and came home.
Q.   Are you very tired after your day out?
A.   Yes, but it was a good day - except I lost my umbrella somewhere.

BRAIN-*friendly* tip:
Add humour to the interview as the questioner becomes a 'very nosey neighbour'.

Unit 9 – World traveller – "Will" - Future (Yellow)

Exercise 1. "Where will you be in May?" and other questions, for example, "How will you travel?" "Where will you stay?" "What will you see?" "What will you do?" "Who will you meet?"

Exercise 2. She'll meet Eskimos at the North Pole. She'll eat rice in China. Yes. She will. She'll be in Kenya in January. She'll visit London/She'll see the Queen.

NOTE:
Students will eventually meet different ways of expressing the future, e.g. *I'll go. I'm going to meet her. My boat leaves tomorrow. We're having dinner together tomorrow.* For simplicity at this stage all FUTURES are YELLOW. When appropriate, explain that one colour (LIGHT BLUE) can sometimes do a job for another, so LIGHT BLUE is working for YELLOW in *We're having dinner tomorrow.*

BRAIN-*friendly* tip:
Discuss your 'dream holiday'. "Where shall we go?. How shall we travel? What famous person shall we take with us?".

TEACHING NOTES

Unit 10   After work - "Going to" - Future (Yellow)

Concept questions: What's Sally doing at the moment? (She's working in an office) What *is she going to do* at 5pm? Where *is she going to have* dinner? etc.

Exercise 1

He's going to finish at 6 o'clock.
He's going to have a drink.
He's going to get changed.
He's going to drive to town at 7 o' clock.
He's going to meet Sally.
They're going to have dinner.

Exercise 2 (for example)

| What's she going to do after work? | She's going to buy a dress. |
| Is she going to walk to town? | No. She's going to get the bus. |

> **BRAIN-*friendly* tip:**
> *Students imagine the scenario as a) the <u>perfect</u> evening for Jim and Sally. What are they going to say / do?*
> *b) a <u>disastrous</u> evening! What's going to happen?*

Exercise 3

What are you going to wear on your date?	Are you going to go home after the restaurant?
Where are you going to have dinner?	Where is Sally at the moment?
What are you going to have to eat?	What time are you going to meet her?

> **NOTE:**
> "Are you going home?" is an alternative.

Unit 11   In my bag ... - "Have got" (Dark Blue)

Exercise 1

After that I've got lunch with the Finance Director.
Sorry. I haven't got time to come. I've got too much work.

> **BRAIN-*friendly* tip:**
> *Take lots of objects and several bags into class. Individual students take turns to make a selection. Their group guesses "Have you got a...?"*

Exercise 2

She's got three. Yes. She's got a gun. She's got a Russian language book.
I've got (for example) a comb, some money, some tissues.

Exercise 3

He's got spots (measles).
No. He's got a broken arm.
He's got a headache.
She's got a bad cold.

Exercise 4

He's got six cousins.
He's got two sisters.
No. She's got a dog.
I've got (for example) one brother, lots of cousins, and a goldfish.

Exercise 5

You've got some cake, a banana, an orange, some yoghurt, a lemon drink – but you haven't got any sandwiches.

Unit 12   Rainbow grammar revision

Side A   (Salty Sue) 1-c (Dark Blue) 2-d (Light Blue)
3-a (Brown) 4-b (Yellow)
(Bazza) 1-b (Dark Blue) 2-a (Light Blue)
3-e (Brown) 4-c (Yellow)

> **BRAIN-*friendly* tip:**
> *Have coloured sweets (Smarties) as prizes for correct answers. Also see if students can make their own 'colour family' for different verbs ('to paint', for example).*

Side B   Exercise 1

What do you do, Salty Sue?	(Dark Blue)
I sold a lot of fish last week, but I didn't sell much yesterday.	(Brown)
What are you going to do this afternoon?	(Yellow)

Exercise 2

No. He's playing computer games.	(Light Blue)
Yes. He did.	(Brown)
Yes. He plays every Saturday.	(Dark Blue)
He's going to play in Russia.	(Yellow)
Do you often play football?	(Dark Blue)
Did you play in the Cup Final ?	(Brown)
Is your team playing well this season?	(Light Blue)
Where are you going to play next week?	(Yellow)

©Brain Friendly Publications   www.brainfriendly.co.uk

I'm David Dark Blue

I paint houses
every day

I'm Lorna Light Blue

I'm painting
my kitchen
at the
moment

I'm Bill Brown

My Uncle Bertie painted

this picture in 1920

I'm Yolanda Yellow

I'm going to paint
that clock tomorrow

Here are four
very important
colour families

Mark Fletcher

The "BIG PICTURE" – 1A

The 'BIG PICTURE' - four "colour families"
Let's talk to Duncan Dark Blue, Lorna Light Blue, Bill Brown, and Yolanda Yellow

Exercise 1

Duncan Dark Blue

Question   What .... you do, Duncan Dark Blue?

Duncan   I .... houses.
I'm a painter and decorator.
My favourite colour is dark blue.

Lorna Light Blue

Question   What are you doing, Lorna Light Blue?

Lorna   I'm .... my kitchen - light blue, of course.

Bill Brown

Question   .... you paint this picture, Bill?

Bill   No. My uncle, Bertie Brown, painted it in 1920.

Yolanda Yellow

Question   What .... to do tomorrow, Yolanda?

Yolanda   I'm .... my clock yellow.

Now connect these sentences to the right pictures, and underline them in the correct colour.

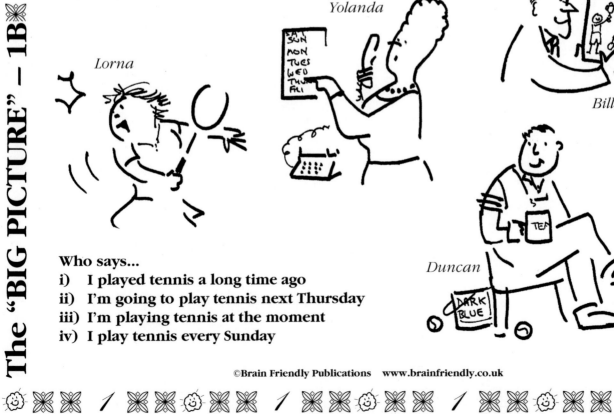

Lorna

Yolanda

Bill

Duncan

Who says...
i)   **I played tennis a long time ago**
ii) **I'm going to play tennis next Thursday**
iii) **I'm playing tennis at the moment**
iv) **I play tennis every Sunday**

Mark Fletcher

My name is Duncan **Dark Blue**

I have two important verbs for **you**

to be   and   **to have**

I .... very tired

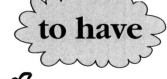

I .... a lot of money

You .... very tall

You .... beautiful eyes

He .... my boss

She .... spaghetti for lunch every day!

We .... good swimmers

We .... too much work

They .... a nice house

They .... very sad

Mark Fletcher

'To be', 'to have' – 2A

'To be' 'to have'

Exercise 1 (to be)

I . . . . very tired.
You . . . . very tall.
He . . . . my boss.
We . . . . good swimmers.
They . . . . very sad.

....

Exercise 2 (to have)

I . . . . a lot of money.
You . . . . beautiful eyes.
She . . . . spaghetti every day.
We . . . . too much work.
They . . . . a nice house.

....

Exercise 3 (to be)

. . . . you tired?   Yes. I . . . .
. . . . he tall?   Yes. He . . . .
. . . . your boss thin?   No. He . . . .
. . . . you good swimmers? Yes. We . . . .
. . . . they happy?   No. They . . . .

....

Exercise 4 (to have)

Do   you . . . . a lot of money?   Yes. I do.
Does she . . . . beautiful eyes?   Yes. She . . . .
    . . . she . . . . roast beef every day? No. She . . . .
    . . . you . . . . a lot of work?   Yes. We . . . .
    . . . they . . . . a nice house?   Yes. They . . . .

....

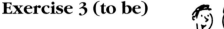

....

All of these sentences are . . . . colour.

Mark Fletcher

Here are two more verbs for you

to go

to like

is a regular verb

I .... to work at 8 o'clock

I .... weekends

Do you often .... to restaurants ?

Do you .... horror movies ?

My brother .... to school by bike

She .... reading

They .... on holiday three times a year

We .... the same things

We .... to the cinema every Friday

They all .... tea

Mark Fletcher

'To go' and 'to like' – 3A

'To go' and 'to like'

Exercise 1 (to go)

I .... to work at 8 o'clock.

Do you often .... to restaurants ?

My brother .... to school by bike.

We .... to the cinema every Friday.

They .... on holiday three times a year.

....

Exercise 2 (to like)

I .... weekends.	So do I.
.... you .... horror movies ?	No. I ....
She .... reading.	So .... I.
We .... the same things.	
They all .... tea.	But I ....

....

Exercise 3

What time .... you .... to work ?	
.... you often .... to restaurants ?	No. I ....
My brother .... to school by bus, he .... by bike.	
.... you ever .... swimming on Fridays ?	No. We ....
How often .... they .... on holiday ?	Three times a year.
I .... horror movies.	But I ....!
What .... she .... reading ?	A science-fiction story.
They .... tea, but they .... coffee.	

....

All of these sentences are .... colour.

Mark Fletcher

When does he…?
Where does he…?
How does he…?

Duncan **Dark Blue's** day…

My day

This is Duncan **Dark Blue.** What does he do on school days?

Exercise 1

Complete the story of Duncan **Dark Blue's** *day. Use these 12 verbs. You will need to use some of them more than once.*

have	get (dressed)	play	arrive
do	go	watch	wake up
get	talk	be (is)	meet

On schooldays Duncan **Dark Blue** *wakes up* .... at 6.30. He .... a wash. After that he .... and at 7.30 he .... breakfast. He usually .... cornflakes, bread, and tea. He ....to school by bike and .... at school at 8.45. He .... lessons in the morning 'til lunch time. Lunch time at school is from 12.30 to 1.30. In the afternoons he .... more lessons or .... sport. He normally .... home at half past four. Mum, Dad and Duncan **Dark Blue** .... dinner at 8 p.m. In the evenings Duncan .... his homework, ... TV or .... his friends. They .... about their plans for the weekend.

Exercise 2

Here are some questions. You write the answers.

What time does Duncan **Dark Blue** wake up?   He wakes up at 6.30.

Does he have a shower?   ....

What does he have for breakfast?   ....

How does he go to school?   ....

Where does he have lunch?   ....

How long does the journey take?   ....

When do the family have dinner?   ....

Exercise 3

Let's change to questions about YOUR day.
Write the answers.

What time do you usually get up?   ....

What do you normally have for breakfast?   ....

Do you usually have lunch at home?   ....

What do you do in the mornings?   ....

Exercise 4

Write 3 more questions so that you can interview a friend.

....

....

....

Underline six sentences on this page in **Dark Blue.**

Mark Fletcher

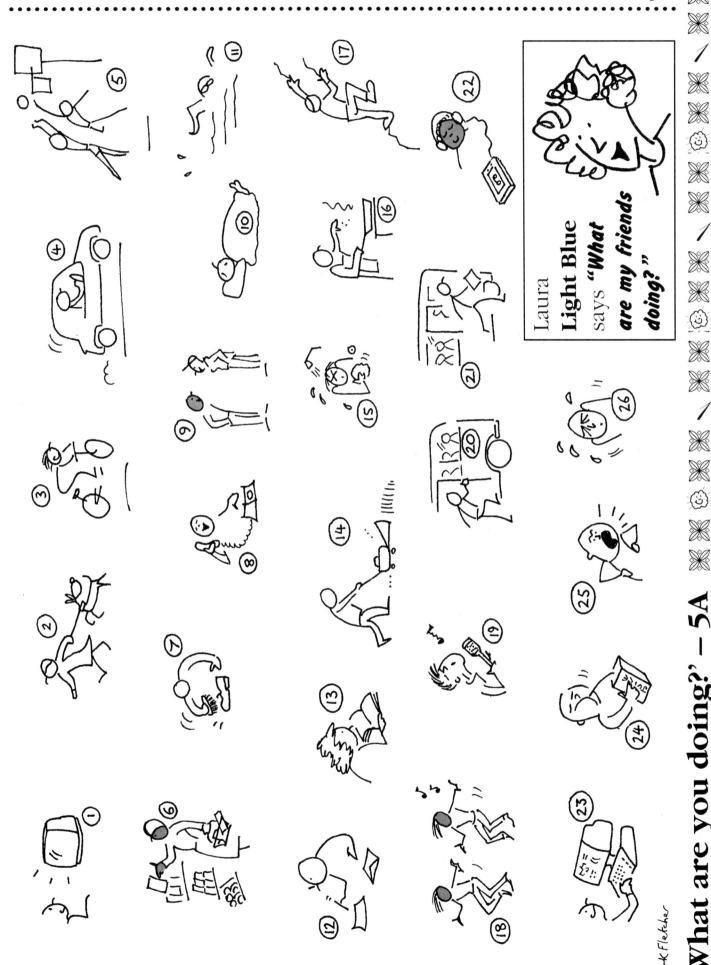

Laura
Light Blue says *"What are my friends doing?"*

'What are you doing?' – 5A

'What are you doing?'

*Lorna **Light Blue** has a very big family. They are very active!*
What are they doing at the moment?

What	am I	**doing?**
	is he (she / it)	
	are you (we / they)	

Exercise 1

Here are 30 verbs. 26 of them are illustrated on the picture page. Fill in the picture titles. Which 4 are not illustrated? Draw your own pictures for them!

climb; talk; get (on); cry; clean; drive; sing; cook; fight; play; cut; take (for a walk); sleep; paint; smoke; have (food or a drink); have (a bath or shower); shout; make (a phone call); watch; swim; use; listen; jog; shop; dance; get (off); ride; write; read

Picture 1   *He's watching T.V.*
2 ....
3 ....
4 ....
5 ....
6 ....
7 ....
8 ....
9 ....
10 ....
11 ....
12 ....
13 ....

14 ....
15 ....
16 ....
17 ....
18 ....
19 ....
20 ....
21 ....
22 ....
23 ....
24 ....
25 ....
26 ....

27	28	29	30

....

Exercise 2

Play the game with friends in the class. For example:
Making Questions.
"What's he doing in picture 19?" "He's singing."
"Picture 3 – Is he riding a horse?" "No. He's riding a bike."

All the sentences are .... colour.

Mark Fletcher

Duncan **Dark Blue** asks … *"What do they do on ordinary days?"*

Lorna **Light Blue** asks … *"But what are they doing on holiday today?"*
At the moment …

Mrs Blue

Duncan

Dagmar

Danny

'Usually, but…' – 6A

Mark Fletcher

'Usually, but.......'

Exercise 1

Danny **Dark Blue** is a fireman. What does he usually do?
He usually wears a uniform. He usually drives a fire engine. He usually fights fires.
But today he is on holiday in **Light Blue** land. He isn't wearing his uniform. He's sitting by a swimming pool.

Dagmar **Dark Blue** is a .... She usually .... a uniform. She
.... sick people. She .... in a hospital. But today she isn't in the
hospital. She is on holiday in **Light Blue** land. What is she doing? ....

Duncan **Dark Blue** .... a student. He .... to school five days a week.
He usually .... hard at school. He .... a lot of books. Is he at school at the
moment? No. He's on holiday in **Light Blue** land. What is he doing? He ....

Mrs. **Blue** .... She .... in a school. She .... English.
She often works in the evenings. But where is she at the moment?
.... Is she teaching? Is she working?
What ....   She ....

Exercise 2

It's a working day today.
Tell me three things that **you** *usually do on a working day.* (**Dark Blue** *things*)

i)   I ....

ii)   I ....

iii) I ....

And what are you doing at the moment? (**Light Blue** *things*)

i)   I ....

ii)   I ....

iii) I ....

....

....

Underline the sentences in the correct colour – **Dark Blue** *or* **Light Blue**.

Mark Fletcher

Bill **Brown's** holiday. He went...

Sunday

Monday

Tuesday

Wednesday

Thursday

Friday

Saturday

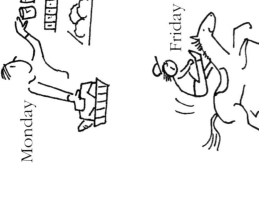

But he also...

GIANT SWITCHBACK

LOCAL SPECIALITIES

PRESENTS GIFTS SOUVENIRS

SUNNY HOTEL

① ② ③ ④ ⑤ ⑥

Bill's holiday – 7A

Mark Fletcher

Bill's holiday

Exercise 1

Let's ask **Bill Brown** *some questions.*
Did you have a good holiday, Bill?

Yes. Last week I went camping on Sunday.
I went .... on Monday.
.... Tuesday.
.... Wednesday.
.... Thursday.
.... Friday.
.... Saturday.

swimming: fishing: climbing: hiking: camping: dancing: jogging: skiing:
horse riding: shopping: skate boarding.

Bill **didn't do** *3 of the things in the box. Which 3 things didn't he do?*

He didn't go ....
He didn't ....
He ....

Exercise 2

Did you do anything else on holiday, **Bill**?
Yes.   i)   I stayed at the Sunny Hotel.
          ii)   I .... some nice food.
          iii) I .... on a giant switchback.
          iv)   I ....
          v)   I ....
          vi)   I ....

Exercise 3

Bill *did a lot of things on* **his** *holiday. Now you write 3 things* **you** *did on* **your** *last holiday.*

i)   ....
ii)   ....
iii) ....

Underline these 3 things in **Brown**.

Mark Fletcher

Bill's holiday – 7B

Betty **Brown** got up early last Sunday…

Betty's day out – 8A

Mark Fletcher

Betty's day out

Betty **Brown** went to London yesterday.

Exercise 1

True or false?
Put a tick in the correct column.

	True	False
Betty had lunch in an Indian restaurant.		
They went to Trafalgar Square.		
She forgot to feed the cat.		
She drove all the way to London.		
She met a friend at the station.		
They bought a lot of presents.		
It was dark when she got home.		

Now you write 5 more statements and
ask a friend if they are true or false.

....

....

....

....

....

Exercise 2

Make questions in the PAST with these verbs.

Did she drive to London?

drive ....   forget ....

read ....   go ....

see ....   say ....

meet ....   get ....

wear ....   buy ....

In pairs ask and answer the questions.

Exercise 3

Write a conversation between Betty and a 'nosey neighbour' about her visit to London.
The conversation should include 6 questions and answers.

*Underline the questions in **Brown**.*

◄ *Draw the 'nosey neighbour'.*

Mark Fletcher

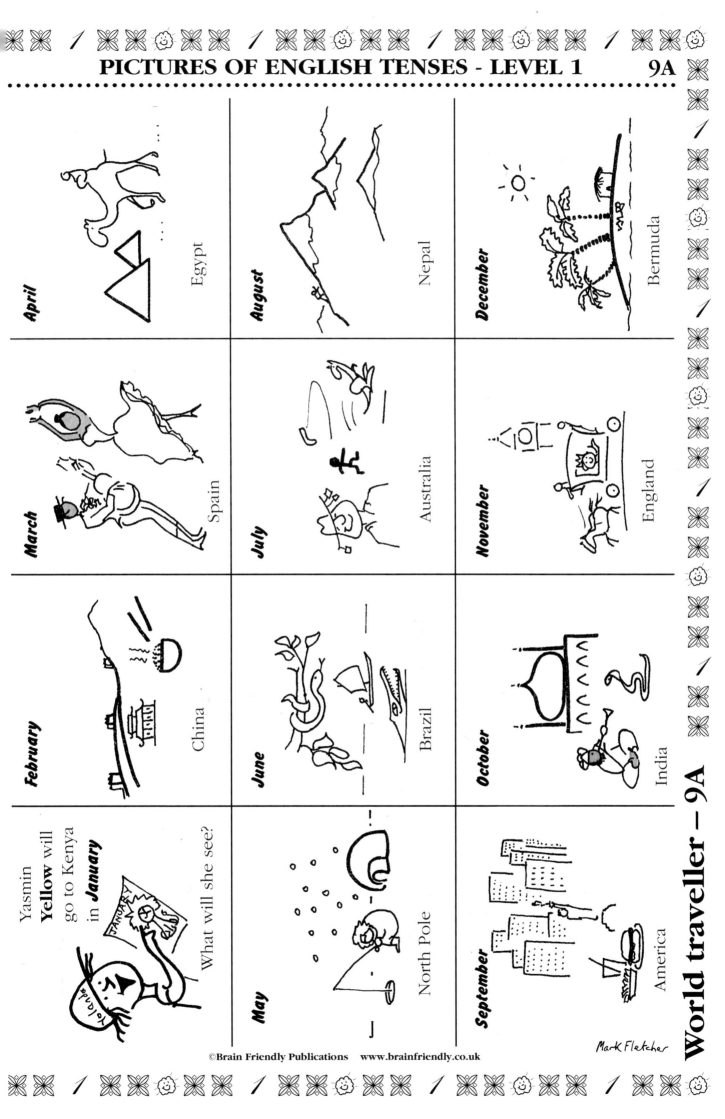

April

Egypt

August

Nepal

December

Bermuda

March

Spain

July

Australia

November

England

February

China

June

Brazil

October

India

Yasmin **Yellow** will go to Kenya in *January*

What will she see?

May

North Pole

September

America

World traveller – 9A

Mark Fletcher

World Traveller

Yasmin **Yellow** is an explorer. Next year she will travel around the world.

Exercise 1

January
  i) Where will you be in January, Yasmin?
     I'll be in Kenya.
  ii) What will you see there?
     I'll see lions.

February
  i) Where will you be in February?
     I'll be in China.
  ii) What will you see there?
     I'll see the Great Wall.

*Ask Yasmin **Yellow** questions for each month.*

March .... March?   *I'll see Spanish dancers.*

April *How will you travel in Egypt?*   ....

May ....

June ....   *I'll travel by canoe.*

July .... July?   ....

August ....

September ....

October .... *beautiful temples.*

November ....

December ....   *I'll lie on the beach and sunbathe.*

Exercise 2

Where will she meet Eskimos?   ....
What will she eat in China?   ....
Will she be in Egypt in April?   ....
When will she be in Kenya?   ....
What will she do in England?   ....

*Underline your answers in **Yellow**.*

World traveller – 9B

Mark Fletcher

It's ..... o'clock now

Jim

Sally

TONIGHT

OFFICE 5 p.m.

7.10

7.30

8 p.m.

6.30

7 p.m.

TOWN CENTRE

Mark Fletcher

After work – 10A

After work.

Jim works in a garage. He's a mechanic. He's repairing a car. He's thinking about tonight because he's going to meet Sally tonight. What's the time at the moment? Where is Sally at the moment ? What's she doing ? What is **she** thinking about?

Exercise 1

Answer these questions.

What time is Jim going to finish work?   ....

What's he going to do at 6:30?   ....

What's he going to do after that?   ....

When is he going to drive to town?   ....

What's going to happen at 7:30?   ....

What are they going to do at 8 o'clock?   ....

Exercise 2

*Now you write 3 more questions - and answers - about **Sally's** programme, and her plans for the evening.*

Q   ....?   A   ....

Q   ....?   A   ....

Q   ....?   A   ....

Exercise 3

Complete this conversation with Jim.

You   ....

Jim I'm going to wear my best suit.

You   ....

Jim We're going to have a good dinner in an expensive restaurant.

You   ....

Jim I'm not sure. Maybe a peppered steak.

You   ....

Jim No. We're going to go dancing after dinner.

You   ....

Jim At the moment ? She's in the bank. That's where she works.

You   ....

Jim At 7:30.

*Underline all the future sentences in **Yellow**.*

©**Brain Friendly Publications   www.brainfriendly.co.uk**

Mark Fletcher

The **Dark Blue** family *have got* a lot of things to tell you.

What has Dora got in her suitcase ?

And for my lunch today …

Debbie's got a busy day.

This is Dougal's family

There are three patients in the doctor's waiting room

"In my bag …." – 11A

Mark Fletcher

"In my bag ....."

*The **Dark Blue** family **have got** a lot of things to tell you.*

Exercise 1

*Let's ask Debbie **Dark Blue** about her day today.*

You	What meetings have you got today, Debbie ?
Debbie	In the morning I've got an appointment with the Sales Director.
	After that ....
	I haven't got any meetings in the afternoon.
You	Would you like to come to dinner this evening, Debbie?
Debbie	Sorry. I ....time to come.
	I .... too much work.

Exercise 2

Dora **Dark Blue** has got some things in her suitcase.

How many bottles has she got ? ....

Has she got anything dangerous? ....

Has she got anything to read ? ....

And you? What have you got in **your** bag?

....

Exercise 3

There are three patients in the doctor's waiting room.

What's the matter with the young boy ? ....

Has the man got a broken leg ? ....

Why is the man holding his head ? ....

The lady is looking miserable. Why ? ....

Exercise 4

How many cousins has Dougal **Dark Blue** got? ....

Has he got any sisters ? ....

Has he got a cat ? ....

Now tell us about **your** family — and other animals! ....

....

....

Exercise 5

What have I got for lunch ? Have I got any sandwiches today?

....

Mark Fletcher

Meet **Salty Sue...**

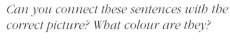

Can you connect these sentences with the correct picture? What colour are they?

a) Last weekend I sold a lot of fish
b) I'm going to sell a lot of fish to the tourists.
c) I sell fish at the harbour
d) I'm selling some fish at the moment

picture 1 -	2 -	3 -	4 -

...and **Bazza!**

Can you connect these sentences with the right picture. What colour are they?

a) He's playing computer games at the moment.
b) He plays football every Saturday.
c) He's going to play in Russia next week.
d) He played in the Cup Final last year.

picture 1 -	2 -	3 -	4 -

Mark Fletcher

Rainbow Grammar – 12A

Rainbow Grammar

Exercise 1

Here are Sue's answers. What are the questions?

You ....?   (Dark Blue)
Sue I sell fish at the harbour.

You Is business good?
Sue Well, I .... a lot last weekend,
       but I didn't .... much yesterday. (Brown)

You ....?   (Yellow)
Sue This afternoon? I hope I'm going to sell a lot more fish!

Exercise 2

....

Is Bazza playing football at the moment?
No. He...............................   (Light Blue)

Did he play in the Cup Final last year?
....   (   )

Does he often play football?
....   (   )

What's he going to do next week?
....   (   )

....

Now ask Bazza the questions....

You   .... (   )
Bazza   Yes. I play every Saturday.
You   .... (   )
Bazza   Yes I did – and we won!
You   .... (   )
Bazza   Yes. The team is playing very well this season.
You   .... (   )
Bazza   In Russia.

....

....

*Write the correct sentence under each picture
– and underline them in the right colour.*

Mark Fletcher

©Brain Friendly Publications   www.brainfriendly.co.uk